I0114440

Secrets the Finance

Industry Don't Want

You to KnowAbout

A Consumer's Guide to Collections

Copyright © 2019 T. Lane

All Rights Reserved

No part of this publication may be reproduced, distributed, or transmitted in any form or by any means, including photocopying, recording, or other electronic or mechanical methods, without the prior written permission of the publisher, except in the case of brief quotations embodied in critical reviews and certain other noncommercial uses permitted by copyright law.

Other Works by the Author

Seductive Dreams 1: The Prophecy Begins

Seductive Dreams 2: The Prophecy Continues

Order Here: Seductive Dreams 1

http://rosedogbookstore.com/seductive-dreams-the-prophecy-begins/

Seductive Dreams 2 (ebook)

http://www.lulu.com/shop/miss-tee-lane/seductive-dreams-2-the-prophecy-continues/ebook/product-23559128.html

Paperback

http://www.lulu.com/shop/miss-tee-lane/seductive-dreams-2-the-prophecy-continues-paperback/paperback/product-23559003.html

Sis, with All Due Respect Shut Up and Listen (Paperback)

www.steelane.com

Also available on ibooks, kindle and nook

<u>*Dedication*</u>

I dedicate this book to:

My Mother, Teni Denise Moore, who taught me to never give up on my dreams and to fight for what is right. R.I.P. Mommy, I love you, and I miss you very much. My Grandparents Geri and LeeVada Moore.

My children, who teach me every day what real love is.

The Creator for waking me up daily, and to everyone that supports my work.

Contents

Moore's Publishing

Certified Publisher

Introduction

I wrote this book because I have watched family and friends suffer from economic whoa. One of the things that affect society as a whole is the ability to obtain and maintain credit. I have more than 15 years' experience in the finance industry, including working for several billion-dollar captive finance companies. So, I can be considered a subject matter expert in regards to finance. My specialty includes collections, negotiations, market research analysis, project management, speech delivery, and working directly with repossession agents. During my tenure, I learned many secrets to the trade. Call after call and customer after customer, I witnessed first-hand how these billion-dollar companies take advantage of their customers. I have been in board meetings with changes being made (after the company had already stolen thousands of dollars from their customers) for them to simply explain that "we are no longer doing it that way." There were no retraction, settlement, or refunds sent back to the customers. I collected millions of dollars from customers that didn't even owe what the companies claimed they owed. I am writing this book to shed light on the unscrupulous behavior of BIG FINANCE. I just couldn't allow myself to continue being part of an industry that knowingly and willingly steals money from its customers.

My wake-up call was the day my department had one of its famous board meetings. I was hired as a negotiator for the company. One of my responsibilities was to get people to pay on significantly delinquent accounts that hadn't yet gone bad. We were told that we were no longer allowed to collect on a separate fee during said meeting. Which was a fee that I had challenged months before this meeting, and I was advised if I did not cooperate with the strategy, I could be terminated. I continued what I was told to do, only to be called into this meeting and be told that what I was saying was correct! And no, they did not say those words at all, not even close. I only used that as a reference so you can understand what had just occurred. I sat there not delving in the moment of being right but more in the moment of being wrong. I had collected millions of dollars on a now considered uncollectible fee when I knew from the very beginning this was something we should not have been doing. However, at the time of my suggestion, my job was threatened if I did not comply. I did what I had to do to keep my job, but I was slowly losing a piece of myself every day I went to work. This is only one instance and one example of BIG FINANCE's behavior, but it happens so much that I have lost count.

I started to lose traction with the company. From that point on, I challenged a lot of what was being told to us by the management team. I was fighting for what was right, but what was right did not help me succeed. That day in that meeting made me realize that I was becoming a part of an unethical industry and somewhere down the line had lost its integrity. These are two qualities that you must have to become an employee with these BIG FINANCE companies. Before you are hired, they give you ethics and integrity exams, and then annually once you are employed; however, BIG FINANCE does not hold themselves to the same morals and values, but I've got them figured out. They only want to hire people with morals and ethics because they wouldn't like what they are doing to be done to them. Wow! That has got to be by far one of the worse things a company can do.

Wow! And Wow! Again. The same thing goes for integrity. This is a prerequisite in getting hired, but it is only to make sure you don't release the secrets that I am revealing to you in this book. I will tell you what I had to do to keep my job and the things these finance companies withhold from you as your right as a consumer. My goal is to bring awareness to the consumer so they know what they are dealing with when it comes to the BIG BUSINESS of finance. If there is nothing else you remember from reading this book, please remember this: READ, and RE-READ your contracts. Your signature is more valuable than you think.

12

Chapter 1. The signing of the Contract

This very well could be the beginning of a significant relationship between you and your finance company, or it could be the worse financial disaster of your life. Now since the basis of my experience is automotive finance, I am delivering you this information based on that premise.Please do your research before you sign any agreement with a finance company. The contract signing happens very quickly, and it is done that way intentionally.

I once read somewhere that decision-making is such a seamless process that we don't realize that we're doing it until our decisions result in unexpected consequences. I worked for a company (that is no longer in business) that financed vehicles with 0% down, 0% interest, and 0 payments for a year. Sounds great, right? Wrong! This was the worst thing that a company could ever do and ultimately led to its demise. The consumer was unaware that after a year of not making payments at all towards their newly financed vehicle, they would have a monthly payment of over $1100 a month for a vehicle that had depreciated approximately $10,000-$20,000. The sales pitch was that after the year is up, just call the finance company and get the vehicle refinanced. When the consumer called into the call center to accomplish this, someone like myself would have to break the bad news that we do not refinance, but they could always seek other lenders. This left the consumer quite confused because the dealership and the finance

13

company both carried the same name. The question most consumers asked was, "why didn't they tell me that?" Their job is to sell cars; their salaries are some-what commissioned based. However, this is not the response I was allowed to provide to our customers. Therefore, I went with the empathy clause, and apologize for the inconvenience. Now, if the consumer took my advice and contacted any other lenders, they ran into yet another challenge. They were kindly informed that since their vehicle had depreciated so much in value from not paying for an entire year, they couldn't issue a $30,000 loan for a vehicle that is now only worth $20,000. In other words, the vehicle was simply not worth it. Literally and figuratively. Now to the average stock market, wall street execs, and finance major, I'm sure they could've seen this coming. However, for the average consumer, this is not common knowledge, and in no way could they have known they would be stuck with a car payment of $1100 a month and a balance owed of about $50,000 on a vehicle that was probably worth about $20,000. This infuriated many consumers, the company did nothing wrong legally, but morally and ethically, they were guilty on all counts. Speaking of, how come we don't have a judicial court system for morals, ethics, and integrity. Seems as though those things only come into play when the government is at risk of losing money.

Anyway, I digress, back to the matter at hand. The consumer signed a legally binding contract and agreed to the terms and conditions set forth. As I mentioned earlier, read, read, and Re-Read your Contract and, most importantly, understand it. This is critical to your future. A finance company can sue you for your commitment to the Contract.

If you have ever been in collections, chances are you may have spoken to me directly. I became one of the top collectors in my industry, being awarded and nominated at company events several times, several years straight. My negotiation skills are a gift, but I don't feel good about the customers that were taken advantage of.

Again, I can't reiterate this enough. Please understand a contract is legally binding. You can and will be held to it. Most contracts are made deliberately to confuse the average consumer; I know this because I have worked directly with my companies' legal team and watched how confusing things can get. In doing my job, I had the opportunity to speak to (what society would call) its elite class. Prominent people such as doctors and lawyers also get taken advantage of during the signing of the Contract. The salesmen are friendly. They offer you coffee, food and will give you just about anything you want as long as you sign on the dotted line. Where have I seen this kind of behavior? Oh yeah! I know! Law and Order. Isn't this the same psychological game the cops play to induce a confession? I mean, they keep people in this little room for hours upon hours. Even though they believe the individual is scum, they manage to look past that and offer cigarettes, coffee, and donuts—anything the person wants. I mean, the similarities are uncanny.

The finance company and the salesman's main objective is to make as much money as they can off of you. It's nothing personal, strictly business, and you must conduct yourself as such when you walk into their facility. They are sharks, and when you walk into a dealership, please know you are in their water. They know more about you than you could imagine. There are consumer reports, surveys, and studies being done on people just like you. The finance companies buy this information to format their sales leads around what you do daily.

So, you must be careful, and if you had done your research on the buying process, you could walk in a little more confident, but this is not something most consumers take advantage of. Most people see a bright red shiny car, and they begin imagining themselves driving it, pulling it into the garage, and showing it off to their friends.

The dealerships know this so, they will even go to the extent of letting you borrow your favorite red sports car of your dreams for a little while, and right there, when they see that sparkle in your eyes, you instantly become prey. The salesman knows what to do, and if he's experienced, he may already have the paperwork drawn up and placed on his desk when he returns from the test drive.

At this point, you sit down, and you are about to sign over the next 3-5 years of your life to a finance company. This relationship is similar to a marriage. It can go well, but if it goes bad is ALL BAD!

The Contract is where your relationship with your finance company begins. You agree to abide by the terms and conditions for the next 3-5 years of your life. Not only is it like a marriage, but some would also compare it to a jail sentence because there is no way out of it other than paying them off along with all the interest that would have occurred. Sounds like a modern-day loan shark. The best way to stay away from the sharks is to keep out of the water. They will never leave their habitat, which sustains their life, so why go to theirs? Given the day and age we live in, that's almost impossible to accomplish. Think of me as your guiding light for financial advice or an insider, so to speak. The people running these businesses may not like what I have to say, but who cares? The public needs to know.

Before you sign any contract, understand the Contract was created by a legal team explicitly designed to protect the company. There is no protection for the consumer. Some may say it's best to bring legal representation before they sign a contract. I say, *"that's not a bad idea."*

I even worked for a company that had a disclosure statement for arbitration already in theagreement. It read like this:

*"**ARBITRATION PROVISION:** YOU AGREE THAT ANY CLAIMS ARISING FROM OR RELATING TO THIS LEASE OR RELATED AGREEMENTS OR RELATIONSHIPS INCLUDING THE VALIDITY, ENFORCEABILITY OR SCOPE OF THIS PROVISION, AT YOUR OR OUR ELECTION, ARE SUBJECT TO ARBITRATION. THIS INCLUDES WITHOUT LIMITATION, CLAIMS IN CONTRACT TORT, PURSUANT TO STATURE REGULATION, ORDINANCE OR IN EQUITY OR OTHERWISE, AND CLAIMS IN CONTRACT TORT, PURSUANT TO STATUTE REGULATION, ORDINANCE, OR IN EQUITY OR OTHERWISE, AND CLAIMS ASSERTED BY YOU AGAINST US, AND THE FOLLOWING COVERED PARTIES: THE LEASE TRUST, AND OR ANY OF OUR OR ITS AFFILIATES AND/OR ANY OF OUR OR THEIR EMPLOYEES, OFFICERS, SUCCESSORS, ASSIGNS OR AGAINST ANY THIRD PARTY PROVIDING ANY PRODUCT OR SERVICE IN CONNECTION WITH THE*

LEASE THAT YOU NAME AS A CO-DEFENDANT IN ANY ACTION AGAINST ANY OF THE FOREGOING. HOWEVER, ONLY A COURT (AND NOT AN ARBITRATOR) SHALL DETERMINE THE VALIDITY AND EFFECT OF THE PROVISIONS BAN ORN CLASS ACTIONS, CLASS-WIDE ARBITRATIONS AND SIMILAR PROCEEDINGS (WHICH APPEARSIN BOLD TYPE BELOW) (THEY "CLASS ACTION WAIVER")ANY ARBITRATION SHALL BE ADMINISTERED BY THIS ADMINISTRATOR JAMS (ITS RULES MAY BE OBTAINED BY CONTACTING 1234 MAIN STREET, ORANGE COUNTY CA 90263). PROVIDED THAT NO ARBITRATION MAY BE ADMINISTERED WITHOUT THE CONSENT OF ALL PARTIES TO THE ARBITRATION BY ANY ORGANIZATION THAT HAS IN PLACE ANY FORMAL OR INFORMAL POLICY THAT IS INCONSISTENT WITH AND PURPORTS TO OVERRIDE THE TERMS OF THIS PROVISION IN ALL CASES, THE ARBITRATOR MUST BE A LAWYER WITH AT LEAST 10 YEARS EXPERIENCE OR A RETIRED JUDGE. SUCH CLAIMS SHALL BE RESOLVED IN ACCORDANCE WITH (I) THE FEDERAL ARBITRATION ACT (THE "faa"),(ii) THE ADMINISTRATORS RULES AND

PROCEDURES IN EFFECT AT THE TIME OF THE CLAIM IS FILED, AND

(iii)THIS PROVISION ANY ARBITRATION HEARING AT WHICH YOU APPEAR

SHALL BE CONDUCTED AT A LOCATION THAT IS REASONABLY

CONVENIENT TO WHERE YOU LIVE THE ARBITRATOR SHALL APPLY

APPLICABLE SUBSTANTIVE LAW CONSISTENT WITH THE FAA (AND NOT

BY ANY STATE LAW CONCERNING ARBITRATION) AND SHALL AWARD

SUCH REMEDIES, IF ANY THAT WOULD BE AVAILABLE IN COURT IF

ARBITRATION HAD NOT BEEN ELECTED. THE ARBITRATOR SHALL

FOLLOW APPLICABLE STATUTES OF LIMITATIONS AND SHALL HONOR

CLAIMS OF PRIVILEGE RECOGNIZED AT ALW AND, AT THE TIMELY

REQUEST OF EITHER PARTY, SHALL PROVIDE A BRIEF WRITTEN

EXPLANATION OF THE BASIS FOR THE AWARD. IF YOU CANNOT AFFORD

TO PAY AND CANNOT OBTAIN A WAIVER OF THE FEES CHARGED BY THE

ADMINISTRATOR OR ARBITRATOR OR IF YOU BELIEVE THAT SUCH FEES

ARE OR WILL BE PROHIBITIVELY EXPENSIVE OR EXCESSIVE, WE AND

THE COVERED PARTIES WILL ENTERTAIN IN GOOD FAITH ANY

REASONABLE WRITTEN REQUEST BY YOU FOR US AND THE COVERED

PARTIES TO PAY OR REIMBURSE YOU FOR ALL OR PART OF SUCH FEES

IN ANY EVENT, IF APPLICABLE LAW REQUIRES US AND THE COVERED

PARTIES TO PAY OR REIMBURSEYOU FOR ALL OR PART OF SUCH FEES

IN ANY EVENT, IF APPLICABLE LAW REQUIRESUS AND THE COVERED PARTIES TO PAY OR REIMBURSE YOU FOR ANY SUCH FEES. SUCH ALW WILL CONTROL. EACH PARTY SHALL BEAR THE EXPENSE OF THAT PARTY'S ATTORNEYS, EXPERTS, AND WITNESSES, REGARDLESS OF WHICH PARTY PREVAILS IN THE ARBITRATION, PROHIBITED FROM PARTICIPATING IN A CLASS ACTION OR PRIVATE ATTORNEY GENERAL ACTION IN COURT OR CLASSWIDE ARBITRATION WITH RESPECT TO ANY CLAIMS WE, THE COVERED PARTIES OR YOU

HAVE ASSERTED AGAINST ONE ANOTHER OR OTHER BENEFICIARIES OF THIS PROVISION. THERE SHOULD ALSO BE NO JOINDER OR CONSOLIDATION OF PARTIES, EXCEPT FOR MULTIPLE PARTIES TO THIS LEASE. IN THE EVENT OF A CONFLICT OR INCONSISTENCY BETWEEN THIS PROVISION, ON THE ONE HAND, AND THE APPLICABLE ARBITRATION RULES OF THE ADMINISTRATOR OR THE OTHER PROVISIONS OF THE LEASE, ON THE OTHER HAND, THIS PROVISION SHALL GOVERN. IF ANY PORTION OF THIS PROVISION IS DEEMED INVALID OR UNENFORCEABLE UNDER ANY LAW OR STATUTE CONSISTENT WITH THE FAA, IT SHALL NOT

INVALIDATE THE OTHER PROVISIONS OF THIS PROVISION OR THIS LEASE, PROVIDEDHOWEVER, THAT IF THE CLASS ACTION WAIVER IS DEEMED INVALID, THEN THIS ENTIRE PROVISION SHALL BE NULL AND VOID SUBJECT TO THE RIGHT OF ANY PARTY TO APPEAL THE DETERMINATION OF INVALIDITY WITH RESPECT TO THE CLASS ACTION WAIVER. YOU AND WE RETAIN RIGHTS TO SELF-HELP REMEDIES, SUCH AS REPOSSESSION OF THE VEHICLE (HOWEVER, THE OTHER PARTY AGAINST WHOM THE SELF-HELP REMEDY IS SOUGHT MAY INITIATE AN ACTION IN COURT ONLY TO ENJOIN THE PARTY FROM USING A SELF-HELP REMEDY. NO MONETARY RELIEF MAY BE SOUGHT IN SUCH A COURT ACTION). YOU ALSO WILL NOT BE SUBJECT TO THIS PROVISION FOR ANY INDIVIDUAL CLAIM BROUGHT BY YOU IN SMALL CLAIMS COURT OR YOUR STATES EQUIVALENT COURT, UNLESS SUCH CLAIM IS TRANSFERRED. REMOVED OR APPEALED TO A DIFFERENT COURT. WITH RESPECT TO ANY CLAIMS COVERED BY THIS PROVISION, A PARTY WHO HAS ASSERTED A CLAIM IN A LAWSUIT OR IN ANY ACTION FOR REPLEVIN IN COURT MAY ELECT ARBITRATION, OR MEY BE REQUIRED TO ARBITRATE, WITH RESPECT TO ANY CLAIM(S) SUBSEQUENTLY ASSERTED IN THAT LAWSUIT BY THAT PARTY OR ANY OTHER PARTY (I.E.S.) IF ANY PARTY ELECTS ARBITRATION WITH RESPECT TO A CLIAM. NEITHER YOU

NOR WE NOR ANY COVERED PARTY WILL HAVE THE RIGHT TO LITIGATE THAT CLAIM IN COURT, TO HAVE A JURY TRIAL ON THAT CLAIM, TO ENGAGE IN PREARBITRATION DISCOVERY EXCEPT AS PROVIDED FOR IN THE RULES OF THE ADMINISTRATOR OR TO PARTICIPATE AS A REPRESENTATIVE OR MEMBER OF ANY CLASS OF CLAIMANTS PERTAINING TO SUCH CLAIM THE ARBITRATOR'S DECISION WILL BE FINAL AND BINDING EXCEPT FOR A LIMITED RIGHT TO APPEAL AS PROVIDED IN THE FAA OTHER RIGHTS THAT YOU WOULD HAVE IF YOU WENT TO COURT MAY NOT BE AVAILABLE IN ARBITRATION. THIS PROVISION IS MADE PURSUANT TO A TRANSACTION INTERSTATE COMMERCE, AND SHALL BE GOVERNED BY THE FAA JUDGMENT UPON THE AWARD MAY BE ENTERED IN ANY COURT HAVING JURISDICTION. THIS PROVISION WILL SURVIVE YOUR FULL PAYMENT OF THE LEASE, OUR SALE OR TRANSFER OF THE LEASE, ANY REPOSSESSIONS OF THE VEHICLE, AND YOUR (OR OUR) BANKRUPTCY."

Wow! Confused yet? I read it, retyped it, and I still don't understand it all. Get this; It's all legal.

Now imagine being presented with this and expected to make a decision in a matter of minutes. It's Ludacris and should be outlawed. The consumer should have the right to have this Contract examined by a legal professional before purchase, but if you even think about trying this one, you will get a response similar to oh! That's our last one, or someone is on the line right now asking about that same vehicle. (The Shmucks) I mean, come on! How is our government even allowing these things to take place? Also, didn't they mention something about the F.A.A.? Is that the same F.A.A. that most people are familiar with? The Federal Aviation Administration? What does the F.A.A. have to do with this Contract? They never really specify which F.A.A. they are talking about. They could be talking about the Financial Administration Act, but isn't that Canadian law? This is just an example of how complex the contract signing process is. I only included this entire Arbitration section to display how extreme signing a contract can be. Again, the Contract is legally binding, and you will be held to the terms and agreement whether you understand them or not. BUYER BEWARE!

Chapter 2: You are late! Pay or Else!

So, now that you have your shiny, brand new sports car, all you have to do is make simple interest payments every month for the next three to five years without fail. Sounds easy enough, right? And I guess if you are financially wealthy and will be the entire three to five years, this may not apply to you. My kind sir or ma'am, you can skip this chapter or come back and read it when and if you do fall behind. There will be some exciting techniques in the next chapter that will expose the call center's deepest darkest secret's

If you are like many members of our community, threats don't go over very well. I have been in call centers and heard how some collectors speak to people that are past due very badly. The _"Pay or Else!"_ approach hardly ever works. If it does, all you've done is frightened an elderly person so much so that they have borrowed on their home, from their pastors, family members, etc., just to keep from getting that phone call again, and in collections, the collector is rewarded for _"Getting the money."_

My approach was much different, which allowed me much success through-out my 15 years in collections. I had empathy with my customers. I understood their situation and financial bind, possibly because I watched my mother struggle financially. Coming from an un-wealthy home always made me want to help versus take away. Yes, I collected lots of money for the companies I worked for, but I was still polite and slow to anger. Of course, I had terrible calls where I was cursed underneath the bus. I even heard words that I had never heard before. I was called names that I wouldn't call my worst enemy, but I kept calm, continued with empathy, and those same customers that called me those horrible names were calling me back, apologizing, and making their payments.

The thing is, most people want to be treated with respect and dignity. No matter what walk of life, they are from. Understanding this notion will make you successful in collections, sales, and customer service. That is, if you want to still be a part of the business after reading this.

The first thing to understand is that you are officially past due after the first date you are late on any contractual obligation. The finance company has a right to repossess their collateral at any point and time you are in default. The only reason they don't come and get their collateral is that they make more money off of you *"when"* you are late. For example, the definition of a simple interest loan (the type of loan most financial institutions use to finance vehicles) is that interest is only calculated on the outstanding principal balance. Simple interest does not compound and increases the loan balance. The amount of interest to be paid for each monthly payment cannot increase. Sounds like a good plan, and I guess it kind of is; however, if and when you are ever late, this will work against you.

Let's start by understanding what interest is. Interest is a fee you pay for using someone else's money (the finance company). This is where finance companies make their money off of you. They are not in the business to just give away money because they think you're cute. They are in the business of making money off of you, so the higher the interest rate, the more money the finance company makes.

When you make your payments to a finance company on a simple interest loan (not leased). The loan is divided into two parts: the interest and the principal. I am going to use this example only because it's the easiest to explain. If your monthly car payment is $500, it is divided into two parts. One-part interest and the other part principal. So, to explain this, let's say you are one of the lucky ones with pretty good credit, and you have gotten yourself a pretty good interest rate. When you send in your $500 payment, the financial institution could pay $250 towards interest and $250 towards your principal balance, but if you have poor credit, you can expect your interest to be more like $300 towards interest and $200 towards principle. This means you will not see a decrease in your principal balance for years to come and more if you are late. Your original Contract has a maturity date and is calculated based on the number of years, the amount you pay, and when you pay. If you default and miss a payment by even just one day, you will pay more in interest. Your payments will go from a normal split of $250 towards principal and interest to more like $400 towards interest, $50 late fee and $50 towards your principal balance, which will, in turn, cost you more money and longer to pay off. Pushing your maturity date right out the window. Don't believe me? Log into your auto loan account and look at the payment history. See how the payments are being applied. Ahhhh…. now you're starting to get it. Now you see how the finance company makes their money.

I can't tell you how many times a consumer has been late on their car payment and get to the last 12 months requesting a payoff or asking when the loan will be paid off. After I complete the calculations, it stirs up an argument, usually with the consumer leading with, "No way, my contract says my maturity date is today, and the loan should be paid off." I love the fact that the consumer has the Contract and did make an attempt to read and understand, but alas, there is yet another misunderstanding. Yes, the consumer is right, and yes, the Contract does have a calculated maturity date, but it's only correct if you've made every payment on time during the entire duration of the loan. That means there were no due date changes, deferments, extensions of any sort, and you were NEVER late. (I will explain each of these in their entirety in the next chapter.) That is the only time the maturity date is relevant.

Every day you are late with a payment, you will pay the finance company more in late fees and interest. To save yourself money try to make your payments on time every single month. The notion the finance company has is that eventually, you will make your payment. That is why they wait at least 90 days to pick up a vehicle. That is three whole months of interest calculated daily, and yes, they do count the weekends. The finance companies have already figured their losses just in case the loan goes bad. They collect more interest at the beginning of the loan; this way, if the loan goes bad, they have already made their money off you. The closer you get to the end of the loan, the less you will pay in interest.

You get it yet? Do you understand how these big finance companies work? They will only lend to you because they WILL make money off of you. Nobody goes to buy a vehicle to get it repossessed. BIG FINANCE knows this all too well.They have researched how consumers pay, and if it does default, they know exactly when it will occur. You get it now? This is how the finance companies make their money and get this; it's all legal. If you ever get into a financial bind and find yourself unable to pay, don't give up. You have options.

First, I would like to discuss how to handle collections calls. I was in the collections industry for more than 15 years, I can say I have seen my fair share of collectors. Some overly anxious collectors go above and beyond to get their guy. I call these guys the movie detective collector. They take skip tracing (locating a debtor) to a whole new level. Not only will they contact your references, but they will also contact your neighbors, contact your co-workers and go to all extremes to make sure they get their guy. This type of collector takes their job personally, and to him, you have just stolen his firstborn child, and when he finally gets you on the phone, he's angry and had to do all the work (that he created all on his own) just toget you on the phone. He's facetious with his words, speaks with a smart tone, and will not allow you to get a word in edgewise. The best way to handle this type of collector is one of two ways. Make up a date you are going to pay, and then when he calls to follow up, come up with a brand- new lie, or you can always just be honest. Telling him exactly what happened and not matching his energy. Eventually, he will have to come down to your level. This type of collector pushes the boundaries. They will have you believe your vehicle is out for repossession and the account is only a few days past due—something most finance companies will not do unless there has been a prior repossession.

The second type of collector is usually the one that is just relentless. Making the same statement several different times, no matter what your response is unless it's Yes, I'll pay today, they completely ignore anything you're saying and continue with their conversation without listening to a word you say. When you get a call from this type of collector, honestly, I have to say. Just hang up. You will not get anywhere with this individual, and you will be more frustrated in the long run.

Last but not least, the firm but a polite collector. Which is my approach and always has been. Explaining to a customer how important their credit has worked wonders for me. Of course, some people say they don't care, but they do. Once I explain that I am sincerely trying to help, then all that changes. My approach has always been to lead with empathy. If you've ever spoken to a collector you liked, I can almost guarantee it was me or someone I've trained.

When I entered the collections world, I noticed how rude and demanding some of the collectors were. Some of them were in the number one spot and brought home thousands of dollars in commission. I vowed that I would never become that person. For some reason, I would reflect on Nicolo Machiavelli, remembering what I had read about him. What resonated with me the most is that famous saying, I'd rather be feared than loved. I would reflect on this and notice how the people around me executed this very poorly. Forcing people to be in fear you isn't going to get them to pay you money. Being a collector does not make you some sort of dictator. Although this may have worked for some individuals but most suffered trying to apply this theory. I decided to do what felt right, which meant talking to people how I wanted to be spoken to, with dignity and respect. This led me straight to the top without even hardly trying. Although at the time, when I was fresh and brand new in my career, I hadn't yet learned the evil things some finance companies would resort to. I was eager to prove myself, and I was incredibly naive. I bit into the company's apple, and they had me for a good while. Eventually, that all changed, and I paid the price.

Chapter 3: Past due? You've got options.

Deferments, Due Date Changes, and Extensions.

So now that we understand the basics of simple finance let's move forward to youroptions.

Let's visit Mrs. Marshall. Mrs. Marshall has fallen behind on her car payment due to a plumbing problem in her home. Below is a scenario that happens quite often in the collections department. To write this book, I have removed the actual steps it took to get Mrs. Marshallon the phone and skipped right to the conversation where Mrs. Marshall answers and explains why she hasn't paid her car payment in over 30 days.

"Hello, can I speak to Mrs.

Marshall?""This is Mrs.*

Marshall."

"Mrs. Marshall, can you verify your address and phone number, please?""What do you mean to verify? You called me?"*

"Yes, ma'am, for verification purposes and to make sure I am not releasing

your personal information to the wrong person, I just want to confirm that I am

speaking to Mrs. Marshall. I am calling from A.B.C. finance about the pink

Cadillac you financed with us."

"Oh yes. My address is 1234 Pretend street, Make Belief

Ca 90222." "Ok, Ma'am, thank you for that."

"We are calling you today because your account is 29 days past due, and as

of tomorrow, this will hurt your credit report. If you make the payment today, we

can prevent the negative credit mark. Currently, the balance due is $500. We have

your bank account on file and can secure your account today."

"That would be nice, but I just done have the money."

"Well, ma'am, if you can tell me the reason you fell behind, I may be

able to offer you some assistance."

"Well, I had a pipe burst here in my home, and it cost me about $1200 to get it fixed. I just wasn't able to make my car payment this month."

"Oh, is that all Mrs. Marshall? It sounds like you have incurred an unexpected expense. If you don't mind sending us an e-mail stating that, I can submit your account for a deferment. You do meet all of the qualifications. You've never had a deferment, and you have made at least 12 payments with us. So, you're already approved. We just need the letter and a check dated by the 10th of next month for your payment that's due tomorrow."

"Sure, if that's all you need, here you go. I have sent it over to you."

"Thanks, so much Mrs. Marshall. I appreciate you taking my call today and if you ever need anything, feel free to give me a call. Here is my direct line."

Boom! That's it. Simple. Now Mrs. Marshall had been avoiding speaking to the collectors for an entire month. She had stressed herself out, wondering what she would do to pay her car payment, and all she had to do was pick up the phone. Mrs. Marshall can now focus more on her plumbing problems instead of worrying about paying two months of past due payments. You, too, could be Mrs. Marshall.

This is just one of the many programs you may qualify for. You just have to know what to say and when to say it. Keep in mind these programs are not set in stone. The finance company makes the rules. This means they can decide who they will give them to and when they will givethem out. For instance, if you are only 1 or 2 days past due. Do not ask for a deferment. You willbe denied. The finance company wants to see you at least try to make the payment before they allow you to skip a whole 30 days. Plus, they are making tons of money during the entire time you are not paying. So, you have to be late before they will even entertain the idea of a deferment, but not so late that it affects your credit. Unless there is some sort of natural disaster (which we will discuss at a later time). You can pretty much give up on getting a deferment while your account is current. You must also have made a minimum of six payments on the loanand six to twelve payments since your last deferral.

Also, keep in mind that a deferment is a temporary adjustment. You still have to make thepayment. It's just paid at a later date. The maturity date will be extended, and the payment will be added to the end of the loan. The benefit of a deferment is to protect your credit and prevent having to pay double payments. You will also continue to accrue interest during the deferral period.

Oh, and I almost forgot most finance companies will allow you to do this at least three times a year, or if you're in a real financial bind, you may request for them to defer 2-3 months at a time!

Moving on to the next option, which is similar to a deferment with a few differences, this attractive option is called a due date change—a DDC in collections terms.

1. With a due date change, you can advance your due date at least 15 days ahead of your current date. For instance, if your car payment is due on the 1st of the month, you can request your due date to be changed to no more than 15 days beyond the current due date. For example, you can ask for your due date to be (at the latest) the 15th of every month. Plus, most finance companies will give you 10 days before they will assess a late fee, so in actuality, you will have until the 25th of every month to make your car payment, essentially buying yourself almost an entire month without paying. The best part of it all, it does not negatively impact your credit score.

2. Before you get all excited and are ready to place that call to the finance

company, you must be current, AND you must not have ever had one before. Unlike adeferment, a due date change can only happen once throughout the loan's entire duration. You must have made your first payment, and you must never have had one before.

Before I go to my final option, let me discuss one minor detail, some finance companies may charge a deferral fee. Somewhere from $25 to $50 for a deferment, which is simply a processing fee, you can sometimes even get this waived. It all depends on yourfinancial hardship.

Ok. Now that we've gotten those two things out of the way. Let's discuss leasing. Whenyou lease a vehicle, you rent a new car for anywhere from one to five years (there goes that prison sentence again).

During the leasing period, you cannot get any scratches on the car, remove any items thatcame with the vehicle, and you must NOT go over the mileage that you agreed on when you signed the Contract. If you do exceed the mileage, be prepared to pay at least 0.25 cents per milethat were exceeded.

With a lease, you have the same options as with finance. Instead of a deferment, you would request what they call an extension. This too could be extended up to 3 months. However,you cannot get 3 months every year. The maximum most finance companies will give you on a lease is three months throughout the entire lease. The reason being is that all of the payments willbe due at the end of the lease. Once your maturity date hits, any extensions that may have been granted during a leasing period will all be due when it's time to return the vehicle. The great thing about leases and extensions is that you won't be paying any interest during the time extension period. You simply pay the payments you didn't pay when your lease expires, and again this is not affecting your credit, and the only thing you may be responsible for is a processing fee—usually no more than $50.

A due date change works the same way as it would with a financed vehicle. You only getone, have made at least your first payment on the account, and you must be current. There's usually no processing fee.

That's it, three simple options—deferment, due date change, and extension. Three optionsyou can exercise when having a genuine financial hardship. Who knew you could skip monthly car payments without it negatively impacting your credit score? Amazing right? I felt the same waywhen I learned about these beautiful tools. The thing is, the finance companies know at some point throughout five years, there will be some sort of financial hardship that may arrive. Whether it be a death in the family, loss of a job, or something like replacing the plumbing,whatever the hardship. Remember! You've got options!

Chapter 4: Still can't pay? You've still got options.

You've been out of work for more than a year, and you've exercised all of your options. You are in the third year of your financed vehicle, and you feel like there is nothing more you can do. You are out of deferrals, and you just used your due date change as your last option to stay afloat. The payment will be expected in the next 15 days, and you do plan to use the extra 10- day grace period. So, you have 25 days to either win the lotto or get some excellent paying job that will give you an advance the same day you start. Since those odds are not likely, I have a few options for you. The first is to refinance. Depending on your credit, you may be able to refinance the vehicle with a lower interest rate and a lower monthly payment. If you are unemployed, this may be a task requiring another income, such as a working spouse or a verifiable home-based income.

Also, you cannot refinance your debt with the same finance company. You will need to seek an outside lender, such as a bank or a credit union.
The second option is to trade in your current vehicle for something much cheaper. This option is a little tricky because if you are driving a Mercedes with a $500 a month car payment and you're lucky enough to find a dealership desperate for sales to pay off your $25,000 Mercedes to put you into a $15,000 Kia Sedona, you will still be responsible for the $25,000. Let me explain it this way. You walk into the dealership and pick out an affordable used vehicle.

You and the salesman discuss that the payments will be no more than $250 a month for the next six years. If you calculate that you're already at $18,000 and the vehicle's price is only $15,000. Then you ask the salesman while he is in a good mood and has already calculated his commission in his head, *"Hey, you think you could pay off my Mercedes for me?"*

He replies, *"Sure, let me see what I can do."*

He then calls your finance company, gets a payoff quote for $25,000, checks your Mercedes' value, comes back, and agrees to pay off your loan for $25,000. Sounds good, right? Sounds like you have out suckered the used car salesman. Well, I am here to remind you that you have not. The used car salesman has just added $25,000 to your new $18,000 loan. So now you owe $38,000 on a vehicle that was initially going for $15,000. What? Did you honestly think that guy was your friend and he was just going to give you $25,000? They have to make it up somewhere, and that somewhere is in the new loan.

I only recommend this as an option if you are at your wit's end and have absolutely no other options at all. This is what the dealership calls being upside down in your car payments. Meaning you owe more than what the car is worth. Everything has its pros and cons. This option is never a good one, but if you are trying to preserve the credit score (you worked day and night ominously to perfect), this may be the best option for you right now.

Eventually, once you are back on your feet, working, and have paid down the balance, you can then trade this vehicle for something else. Time is your only friend when you use this option.

Option number three. Bankruptcy. Just the mere mention of the word sends chills down your spine, doesn't it? Well, don't be afraid of the word Bankruptcy. Our current commander and chief, the President of the United States of America, Donald Trump, filed Bankruptcy 4 times under the corporation's names. Although these are not personal Bankruptcy, there's still much to say about Bankruptcy in general. Don't be afraid of it. It's America's way of saying, "Ok, you tried, and you messed up somewhere down the line, let me help you." Accept it and do it. If it's an absolute must.

I filed my own personal Chapter 7 bankruptcy in 2014. I filled out my paperwork, I represented myself in court, and I got my Bankruptcy discharged. Before my Bankruptcy was discharged, I was already getting advertisements from Honda Financial saying I qualified for a brand-new car with my Bankruptcy. They had a unique program specifically for people in my situation. Something I had no idea about until I filed.

When dealing with the whoa of financial ups and downs, the best thing to do is remain positive no matter the outcome. We live in America. A place where you can get outof debt and back into debt with the same organizations that you didn't pay the first time around. Relax, take a deep breath and understand that just because you have a temporary setback does not mean there are no solutions. Bankruptcy is temporary. They make it sound like it's a lifesentence when they say, "It will stay on your credit for 10 years." Ok, so…and??? Didn't it take me just about that same 10 years to get into debt? I think the 10-year mark is not so bad. Besides, what am I missing, really? Sure, I'll be paying a higher interest rate for the things I want, sure I may not get an American Express card right away, but shouldn't this be the case anyway. If I'm filing for Bankruptcy, obviously, something has gone wrong, and I don't need anything more than what I am qualified for anyway.

So, if need be filing the Bankruptcy, get out of debt, and move on.

The most popular personal bankruptcies are Chapter 7 and 13. They both depend on how muchyou owe and what your intent is. Chapter 13 bankruptcy is considered a debt consolidation. You keep your items, notify the finance companies you have filed chapter 13. They must reduce your monthly payments, then you make a payment directly to the trustee's office who sends your finance companies a check every month.

See simple and easy. Isn't that a relief? All you have to do is make one payment to the trustee's office every month for a lower amount, and you have saved yourself so much stress and found a little piece of heaven.

Thank me later, or now is a good time. I accept all donations and personal thank-you e-mails. Let's discuss further chapter 7 bankruptcy, which is what I filed. Again, very simple.

They even have an option of giving your vehicle back and having the debt erased or keeping your car with a reaffirmation and making smaller monthly payments. Isn't that great? I mean, I don't know why Bankruptcy has such a negative connotation. I get it. It shows that you were irresponsible with money at some point in your life, but aren't we all? If everyone was responsible financially and never had any hardship, then the statistics wouldn't be what they are today.

According to The A.B.I. (American Bankruptcy Institution) reports that in California alone, so far up to July of 2019, 40,241 Californians have filed for Bankruptcy. With a ratio of 76% being chapter 7 and 23% being chapter 13. Feels better right? Knowing you are not alone in this. I get it Bankruptcy is not something you want to do, but if it's something you need to do, then just do it, my friend. Give yourself a brand-new start. Getting all of your debt erased and starting over is not so bad. Take it from me— someone who has done it and lived to talk about it.

Chapter 5:

Voluntary or Involuntary

So, … You've gone through all of the procedures already discussed except for filing Bankruptcy. Either you're just not sure it's the thing for you, or maybe you've already filed and simply can't do it again. Whichever the case, you have decided to give the vehicle back to the finance company. This is what we as collectors call a voluntary repossession. It's when you Mr./Mrs. Pleasant customer calls the collections department and says, "Hey, come and pick up my car. It's sitting down the street with the keys under the mat." Ah…I know what you're thinking. Keys under that mat? Yes, this was the process, and surprisingly so, none of the vehicles were ever stolen.

Anyway, I digress, back to the matter at hand. You've placed the call, and the representative goes over all of the significant factors with you. Instead of explaining it to you, I'll use a scenario that happens all the time in the collections department.

As a matter of fact, it's procedural.

"Hello, thank you for calling A.B.C. Motor Credit. My name is NaTisha how can I help you today?"

"Hi, NaTisha! My name is Bill Smith, and I'd like to return my vehicle. I live at 7894 W. New Hampshire Ave. New Angeles Ca 123456."

"Ok. Thanks for that information, Mr. Smith." "Can you also verify the last four digits of your social security number so I can make sure I am speaking to the correct person?"

"Sure!" "Who else other than myself is going to call in and surrender MY vehicle?""Anyway, it's 0033."

"Thank You, Mr. Smith." "So, I understand you would like to surrender your vehicle to us. Can you tell me why?"

"Yes, NaTisha, of course, I can." "I've been out of work for more than a year now, and I simply can't afford to make the payments. "You guys have given me three deferments and a due date change, and still I just can't continue to make the payments at $500 a month. "I've also triedto refinance, but my income to debt ratio is just too high at this time." "I've borrowed from family and friends; I just need you to come and pick it up."

"Ok, Mr. Smith." "I understand. I can set up a voluntary surrender for you, but there are afew things I must make you aware of."

"First, I have to tell you that repossession will stay on your credit for 7-10 years. Whether it be voluntary or involuntary, it affects your credit in the same manner." "The only difference isthe repossession cost will only be $350 instead of the normal $400." "This amount will be addedto your deficiency balance."

"The deficiency balance is the amount you will still owe A.B.C. Motor Sales after yourvehicle is sold at the auction. A cost that you too will incur."

"For example, your current balance on your loan is 20,000, we will pick up the vehicle and sell it at the auction, but first, we will add the repossession fees and auction fees to your loan.""So, your balance will be about $21,050."

"The Kelley blue book values your vehicle at about $10,000." "If we can get this amountat the auction, it will be applied to your loan." "You will owe approximately $11,050. This amount will be due and payable as soon as you receive the notice. If it is not paid in full, A.B.C. Motor Sales reserves the right to exercise all options, which can lead to wage garnishment, judgments, liens placed against your property, and all other collection procedures."

"Mr. Smith, do you understand what I have just explained?""Yes."

"Would you still like to proceed with the voluntary surrender?""Yes!"

"Ok." I will submit the request today and have our agent contact you for a date and timeto pick up the vehicle."

"Thanks for calling A.B.C. Motor sales." "Have a great day."

Wow! Mr. Smith took that pretty easy. No rebuttal. No argument. He was the perfectcustomer. Or, wait. Was he?

Let's dig a little bit into Mr. Smith's finances. Reviewing notes on the account, it seems he was out of work for some time, but there's also an inquiry on his credit report for the Lamborghini dealership as of a month ago. There are a few things that could have happened here. Mr. Smith could have been just browsing and looking for a new vehicle, or he could have just purchased a brand-new Lambo. Let's go with the latter. Let's pretend that Mr. Smith just bought a brand-new Lamborghini and has it parked in the driveway of the new home he just purchased in Calabasas. Because collectors have access to public records and data systems, let's say Natisha was a little suspicious of Mr. Smith and figured he was just taking this too lightly. She decides to run a public record search and has found that Mr. Smith has filed for Chapter 13 Bankruptcy and has included all of his debt. Including the brand-new Lambo parked in the driveway of his home in Calabasas.

Yes, this is what people do, and yes, it is all legal. Now don't get me wrong, I am not telling people to defraud the system. I am saying that if your income qualifies and you meet the criteria, then these options are available to you. I mean, really, what can anyone do? Once you file Bankruptcy and it's discharged, your debt is wiped away. Erased!
Gone! Finito! As I mentioned before, it's a brand-new start—a chance to get it right the second time around.

I have seen this happen time and time again. I have spoken to individuals from all walksof life. From secretaries, school teachers, perfume salesmen, to wall street execs, doctors, lawyers, stockbrokers, and guess what? The second group of people all call in with the same demeanor as Mr. Smith. They what to do with their money and what not to do. They understandthe programs that are available to them, and they take full advantage. I believe this is why they are successful even when they don't have a job. They know the secret's that many people do not.

Now onto an Involuntary repossession. It is more common in a collector's world than anything else. These are fun. Not because you are takingsomething away from someone, but because you are on a search and rescue mission.

We use the term "skip-tracing" when a customer has gone off the grid with our vehicles while in collections. I will again use a semi-factual situation.

"Hi, can I speak to Randolph Stiller, please?""This is Randy." "How can I help you?"

"Hi Mr. Stiller, this is NaTisha from A.B.C. Motor Sales. I was following up with you regards to your account on the Range Rover." "Currently, we show the account to be 90 days pastdue and has been set up for repossession." "The past due balance is now $4000. Can we set up a payment today to bring the account current and get you out of the repossession status?"

"No!" "You can't." "I haven't paid you, I'm not going to pay you, and I hope your company goes belly up." "A.B.C. Motor Sales lied to me from the very beginning of this loan." "The dealership said one thing, and now the finance company is saying the opposite." "I'm notgiving you anything." "If you want the car, find it yourself."

"Hello, Mr. Stiller, are you there?" "Hello, ???"

Ok. So obviously, Mr. Stiller has now hung up on NaTisha. Now her job has gone fromcollector to skip tracer. Skip tracing (as explained earlier) is what the finance companies do to locate a vehicle no longer located at the address provided.

Natisha will now call all the references on the Contract and send an agent to visit all addresses known to the debtor. While the agent is out in the field, she will also be calling neighbors, running associate searches, and looking for any family members that have been known to have a close relationship with the debtor. At this point, NaTisha has become an overnight detective. She is no longer looking for the debtor. She is not looking for the peoplecloses or who were the closest to them. This process has a 90% success rate.

Natisha finds an address to Mr. Stiller's mother, calls the agent, and provides the address. The next morning when NaTisha gets into the office, there is a voicemail waiting for her from therepossession agent stating they "popped" the vehicle last night at 2 a.m. at the debtor's mothers' home.

There's also a voicemail from the debtor. I will let your imagination decide what youthink the voicemail said.

Now the finance company is back in possession of the vehicle with a past due balance of $4000. The process will be the same as voluntary. It will be sold at the auction, and the fees will be attached, but they will be much more than a voluntary repossession. Since Mr. Stiller decided to hide the vehicle, it took several skip tracings tools and actions to locate him. He has now racked up more than $1000 in skip tracing fees. A letter is sent to him advisingof the deficiency balance, when and where he can get the vehicle back. Getting the car back is an option if Mr. Stiller pays all of the money he owes plus the repossession costs. However, since he skipped with the company's vehicle, he is no longer trustworthy and doesn't qualify forreinstatement.

The vehicle is sold at the auction, the company sends a deficiency balance letter. Mr.

Stiller never responds and months later receives a $500 a month garnishment.

The point of both of these scenarios is, there is an art to beingin collections. The fact is nobody wants collectors calling them. Nobody wants to be past due, but ifyou find yourself there, you must make the proper decisions that are well thought out to save yourself from future headaches.

If you compare Mr. Smith's situation to Mr. Stiller's, you can clearly see that Mr. Smith knew something Mr. Stiller didn't. Mr. Smith may have been upset with the finance company for the same reasons Mr. Stiller was, but Mr. Smith will not get garnished whenhe decides to go back to work. There's an art to being a debtor. If you ever find yourself in debtover your head. Please be aware that you have options, and I will be glad to discuss them with you.

Chapter 6:

Skip Tracing.

Now we touched a little on skip tracing in chapter five, and I explained how collectors locate a customer who has "skipped" with their vehicle. I will give you some inside information about how this works, and it will blow your mind. Remember back in chapter five when I said I had a customer leave me a voicemail once his vehicle was repossessed. Well, his account is what we called a skip; it was explicitly assigned to me because I was good at locating individuals that didn't want to be found. A skip tracers' job is similar to that of a detective because they know the person is hiding and evading themand have to catch them where they think no one will ever find them. I've seen people in locations they believe no one would ever look. I once located one of our vehicles at a customer'sgirlfriend's house. This sounds pretty obvious, right? The only problem is he was married, and when he found out we were looking for him at his girlfriend's house, he immediately called andpaid the account in full.

Before I dive into the beautiful world of skip tracing, I'd like to give you an idea of the personality that comprises a person to become a collector. Please understand collectors get paid very well to do what they do and even better if they are the best. For instance, when I first startedin collections, I only had a high school diploma, and I commanded $18 an hour. That may not sound like much today, but the year was 2000, and I was about 20 years old with no kids. Thiswas good money. Today's collectors can command $25 an hour (depending on experience) plus a bonus opportunity of anywhere from $500-$1000 a month, depending on the company and how big their portfolio is. I wanted to provide this bit of information because I have had customers flat out tell me that I was a low-level employee only making $10.00 an hour. There's nothing wrong with that, but I just want to clear up the misconception that collectors are low-level employees. They are not, and most of the time, I was making more money than the people I was collecting on, which included a list of pretty high-profile individuals who seemed to have it all with their doctorate and attorneys' degrees. Yet here they were in collections, unable to pay their care payment. Go figure!

The collections and sales team are incredibly similar. The company relies on the sales team to bring in a profit, and they rely on their collections team to reduce loss. A collections department can make or break a business, which is why the company invests in them so well. There is much money invested in training, re-training, testing, and skill improvement to ensure the collections department has the best tools necessary to execute their daily job functions.

Ok. Now you understand a little bit about the person who is calling you every day 3-4 times a day regarding your past-due car payment. Collectors are self-motivated, driven, aggressive, self-starters, ambitious and goal-oriented. They are ready for their name to be called at the next company meeting and have had their eye on that top collector trophy that's going to be awarded. I have these same qualities, which is why I was so successful in my career. I rubbed noses with V.P.'s and delivered speeches at companies' functions. I was the all-star of my team. When I exceeded all goals and expectations, I was awarded a relocation package to continue my work to increase production in our eastern region.

Now, back to that voicemail message the customer left me that had skipped with our vehicle. I can't quote the explicit content, so I will summarize what was left, and it was something like this, *"I swear if I ever find you, see you or meet you, I am going to mess you up real bad." "I hope you burn in hell for what you did." "I paid you and you still took my car!" "I am going to sue you and the company." "You had no right sending a repo agent to my mother's house." "Who do you think you are?" "I am going to find you." "I know exactly where you are located and I am going to blow the whole building up!"*

This carried on until he used all the time on the recording. I hit delete and yet another message with him ranting and raving about the terrible things he was going to do to me and the company. I deleted that message too. Then my phone rang, I answered, and yes, it was him, yelling and screaming about how he wanted the rims off of his vehicle, the money back for the T. V's he put in the headrests, and the $1500 check that he already sent it. I let him go on and on, and then I promised to send him the check back. He was still upset but seemed a little relieved that I was listening and honoring at least one of his demands.

Now I bet you are wondering how I found him. So, what we know so far is that I found him at his mother's house. That sounds like the first and easiest place to find someone, but in this case, it wasn't. He was a grown man and lived on his own for quite some time, had a stable job for a few years, and didn't even have his mother listed as a reference or an emergency contact. His mother was not the usual suspect.

It took me a few weeks and some good old-fashioned gumshoe detective work to locatethis individual. First, I pulled his application. I called all three references he provided, and all three numbers were disconnected.

Next, I called all the caller I.D. numbers he had called us from and reversed searchedthose same numbers for addresses. There was one number that I called. It irritated the woman so much, I knew she would be useful at some point, but I didn't stop there. I called past employers,sent an agent to the last known address, and left messages with a few of his associates. I was coming up short.

Lastly, I decided to focus solely on the woman who was extremely irritated with me calling her home and asking for this individual. I had a gut feeling that either she was his girlfriend, ex-girlfriend, or his mother. And Yup! You guessed it—good old mommy, dearest. I remember the 3rd and final attempt I made contacting her was the one that told it all. I asked to speak to the customer, and she responded angrily, saying, "I told you, he doesn't live here, has never lived here, and I don't know where he is." She abruptly slammed the phone down and hungup in my face. There was so much emotion involved, she gave herself away.

I called my repossession agent, and I told him to get the car from the address that matched the phone number. When the agent called the next morning, he stated he found the vehicle at our customers' mother's house parked across the lawn. He described the car as being heavily modified. And that's when I realized why the customer was so upset about us repossessing his vehicle. He had probably spent well over $10,000 on the car and was nowunable to make the payments.

This was just one instance of how skip tracing works. My tactics were ethical and never involved any underhanded business, but I have seen and known people to do things illegal and unethical. I once worked with a girl who would get a borrower's address and call all the neighbors until she got one on the phone that knew the customer or just bold enough to knock on the customers' door and tell them the car finance company was on the phone. I wasbeside myself when I would hear her doing this. I asked her once, "Is it ok for us to do that?" Sheresponded, "Nobody told me anything." I could only shake my head in disgust.

The method of skip tracing is a very delicate tool. You have to be smart and know the laws of the state you are calling. Collectors before my time harassed and threatened consumersso much that a law had to be created to prevent collectors from operating with unscrupulous behaviors.

I remember another time when a collector got so upset about being yelled at by a customer that she used her skip tracking tools to find our customer's current address. On herlunch break, she called the customer back, cursed her out, and threatened her by telling her the address she had found. This individual was immediately terminated when management found out.

Skip tracing was fun for me. I loved it. The best part is that it didn't always end up in repossession. Most of the time, people were so unnerved by someone from the finance companyshowing up at their doorstep that they immediately whipped out the check, sometimes cash, andmade the payments.

Please also keep in mind any type of skip tracing involved in locating a customer; whatever the fee incurred is added to the customers' loan. Yes, you heard me right. You are paying when a finance company has to locate you to pay your bill, and as I mentioned earlier, it's all in the Contract that you signed when you had those big eyes set on thebeautiful red car.

Chapter 7:

Deficiency Balances and Negotiations

I once had a customer tell me, "To go Fly a Kite," at the time, I had no idea what it meant. I knew it was an insult, but go fly a kite? I was utterly perplexed about the insult. What did it mean to tell a person to go fly a kite? I asked a few of my co-workers and quickly found out what it meant. My response was, why didn't he just say that? I bring up this scenario because some things we know and somethings we don't. We know some things because they are taught to us from our parents, brothers, sisters, aunt and uncles, and other things we pick up along the way. I think negotiation is a little bit of both. You take the things you already know and apply them to the things you have learned along the way. There is an art to negotiation, and you have to be willing to walk away before you give the house away.

So, this is the process, an account becomes 90 days past due, it's then repossessed, sold at the auction, the amount it sold for is subtracted from the balance you owe, and you are sent the final deficiency balance letter. This is the amount you must pay to prevent the finance company from suing you. If they are successful in suing you, not only is there a repossession on your credit for 7-10 years, but you now have a public record reporting for the same period of time, but if you negotiate, you can avoid the legal action and focus on getting the repossession removed from your credit report at a later date. For now, were going to focus on paying the deficiency balance.

Before you call the finance company, all Willy-Nilly with $5000 in your hand because that is the amount they said you owe. Let me give you a few pointers in negotiation. First, pleaseknow the finance company has already considered your balance a loss, and any amount they get from you will be a profit, but even in this, they still have a number they will not go under. Second, if you call to pay your deficiency balance, you have just made the collectors day, week, month, or hell, maybe even their year. The collector is excited to speak to you, but hewon't show it at all if he's good.

If you play poker, then I am sure you know this tactic all too well. If you don't andnegotiation is not your strong suit. Let me give you a few pointers.

1. Do not tell the collector how much you have and a low you are willing to go. This is ahuge mistake, and the collector will smell it. Remember, you can never go lower than ahigh number, but you can always go higher than a low number.

2. Don't fall for the old "this is my final offer trick." It is not, and the collector will usethose exact words.

3. When the collector finally says, well, there isn't much we can do. Tell him ok andhang up. Do not call him back. Allow him to sleep on it and call you back. I can guarantee he will tell you he spoke with his supervisor, and he could get theprice lowered for you.

4. The 3rd or 4th attempt of negotiating or at the end of the month, you are guaranteed an excellent deal.Every collections department across the united states closes its books at the end of the month. Use this to your advantage to get that $5000 deficiency balance knocked down to half.

5. Finally, once it's paid and you have your settlement letter. Allow it to be reported tothe credit bureau's then call and dispute it and have it removed from your credit report. Simple right? I bet they didn't teach you this in your economics class.

Thank me later. On second thought, thank me now. I'm on Instagram as missteelane. Facebook as T. Lane.

Chapter 8:

3rd party collectors. The bottom feeders

Third-party collectors, like agencies and law firms, are entirely different than the collectors that work for the finance companies directly. They make significantly less money. I found myself working for one of these companies. I had been laid off from my great job at the tremendous captive company that I worked for, and I had a friend who was fired (for smoking weed at work on the clock before it was legal) tell me she could get me in she worked. Yes, I knew her history, yes, I heard about this law firm, and yes, I was skeptical, but I also had a three-year-old and a husband adding pressure, so I went on the interview un-shockingly got the job the same day.

When I showed up to work, I noticed the people I worked with were not like me. Some of them had just gotten out of jail the day before. Others were fresh out of rehab. The first week I was there, my friend that referred me to the job had money stolen right out of her wallet. Can you believe that? Someone walked over to her desk, went into her purse, and stole a $100 bill right out of her Louis Vuitton back. Something like this would never have happened at the places I had worked at before. I had never seen a group of people more scandalous in my life, and I have lived in some pretty dangerous places.

This place was like a zoo, without the zookeeper. The department manager was a guy that didn't even work directly in the office, but he made his presence felt. He reminded of that movie with Denzel Washington where the little girl was kidnapped, and he ends up getting in contact with the boss who put in the order. No one had ever met this boss, and no one knew how he was. All they knew was "la Voz."

This was my nickname for our boss. He would pull our numbers every day, and if your numbers were bad, your supervisor would come to your desk and say, "La Voz," wants to speak to you. It was the most terrifying thing in the world. I kept placing myself in that movie with Denzel feeling like I was working for a murdering maniac.

The first time I was told "la Voz" wanted to speak to me, I remember my heart racing and my palms sweating. I had to dial a unique extension from my phone to get to him. I remember him saying to me. "Ok, it's been 30 days. I expect your numbers to increase. If not, we will be having a different conversation." I nervously hung the up phone , stepped outside with my friend, and asked her what I should do. She said, "Sh**, get yo numbers up." Something so simple to her. Now here I was, a top collector, negotiator,team lead who never had a problem collecting money from any of my customers but couldn't make it in 3rd party collections. This was a different ball game, and eventually, I was cut from the team.

As a third-party collector, your job is to collect on bills people have already refused to pay, have forgotten about, and or have already cursed out several different agencies and told them they will never pay. I came along with the firm but thepolite approach and was missing my goal consistently. Because I am always looking for ways to improve, I'm incredibly competitive, and I sincerely believe there is nothing on this planet anyone in the world can do better than me. If you can do it, I can do it better. Period. So, I decided to sit with the people that we're "doing it." In case I forgot to mention it, these collectors get a commission that is solely based on their performance. They also get an hourly wage, but it's not very much, so bonusing is vital for them to pay their rent, car payment, and the 22" rims they had on their cars. I mean, some-how, these guys were making a lot of money.

So there, I am sitting next to someone who bonuses month after month and will soon be promoted to supervisor. I listen in on my 3-way headset connected to his phone, and I can hear everything he and the customer are saying. The way he spoke to them and the things he was saying were things that would have never been allowed at the companies I worked for. He threatened these consumers with deportation, wage garnishment, using intimidation tactics, bullying, and flat-out lying to people who didn't know any better.

After a day of training with him, I went back to my desk and felt very sorry for the people who had to deal with this guy. The next day the company sat me with someone worse than the first guy. This guy used curse words and left voicemails for customers releasingall of their past-due information. This was the worse, and from that day forward, I knew this wasn't the place for me, but I couldn't quit. I still went to work every day. I began tohelp the people I was speaking with. If I knew there was a garnishment in order, I wouldcancel it. If I knew there was a way to get the account sent back to its originator, I did. Ifthere was any way I could help these pure abused customers, I did. I remember rejecting an account from a major phone company because the customer was 80 years old. The customers' granddaughter had stolen her information and got a phone in her name.

I sent the account back to the client as uncollectable. This went on and on for about a month. Then I got the call. You guessed it, "La Voz." My supervisor came out of his office and told me to call "la Voz." I was questioned about my numbers. I responded with, "I don't know, the boss; I'm doing all I can." He said, ok, and that was the last time I ever spoke to "la Voz." My supervisor called me into his office. I asked if I needed to bring anything, he said, you can get your purse. I knew right then I was getting fired, and to say the least, I was pleased about it. My supervisor sat me down and was at a loss for words. He said, "Tanisha, we all like you here, and we want you to stay. We love your personality, and we think you are a great person, but your numbers are getting lower every month instead of getting higher, and "La Voz" has already made his decision. I told him I understood, shook his, and thanked him for the opportunity. I had never been so happy and so sad at the same time. I was happy I never had to work for these bottom feeders again, but I was also sad about losing income. Although it wasn't much, it was keeping the gas and the lights on. Now that I think back on it. They did me a huge favor. If I had stayed at thatplace any longer, I might have turned into one of them. "La Voz," if you are reading this, thank you very much. Not only did you do me a personal favor, but you've also contributed to a chapter in this book. Thank You!

If you decide to make a payment to these bottom-feeders, please do so without providing your bank account information. I recommend a pre-paid card with only the amount on it in which you intend to spend. I would not offer them any more than 20% to settle the debt. They will just about take anything at this point. Also, make sure you get your paid in full letter or settled in full letter before you get off the phone with them. I have seen instances where the representative agreed upon an arrangement, and thecustomer pays the balance with a promise for their credit to be updated, and the credit never got updated. Getting these kinds of letters is vital to getting your credit report updated.

Once you receive your pad in full letter, send it to the credit bureaus immediately. Working with the 3rd party collectors can be beneficial, but you have to be careful withthem, don't trust anything they say, and get it all in writing.

Chapter 9: Bankruptcy

Bankruptcy seems to be a touchy subject for some. I noticed that the word puts people in a state of fear, and I'm not sure why. Bankruptcy was designed for the Americans who get behind in their bills and can no longer afford the lifestyle theyonce sustained. However, people are extremely reluctant to even consider the idea. A bankruptcy will stay on your credit for seven to ten years, but it eliminates your debt and allows you to start over again and get it right the next time. The most common types of bankruptcies are chapter 7 and chapter 13. It is a common misconception that you have toowe a minimum amount to file. This is not true, but how much you owe needs to be considered approved for the debt to be discharged. If you are unemployed and overwhelmed with debt, it may be a good idea to file.

Just because you file, Bankruptcy doesn't mean you are free and clear. Your file still has to be reviewed by a judge, and your filing can be dismissed. If the judge finds thatyou can pay your debt yourself or have other means of paying, your Bankruptcy could be dismissed, and even in the event of dismissal, you can still file an appeal.

If it is proven you cannot afford to pay your lenders, the judge will discharge your debt and provide you a case number. It's that simple. I filed my chapter 7 bankruptcy all on my own, without an attorney and paralegal. I did a quick google search, downloaded the software, followed the necessary instructions, and get this; I kept my car and continued making payments. With all of my debt cleared, I was able to continue making my car payments. This wasa great relief because I needed my car to get my kids back and forth to school.

Once you receive your case number, it is essential to provide this information to your creditors. Even if you keep your car and you decide to continue making payments.Once you provide your creditors the case number, they can no longer collect on the debt you owed them. Even if you decide to keep your car and make payments. The creditor cannot collecton your account if you fall past due, but they do have the right to repossess their vehicle if they deem it necessary, but they cannot sue you for the deficiency balance once the car is repossessed. In my opinion, filing Bankruptcy is by far the best option you have when you are completely drowning in debt. If you can't pay it, you can't pay it— no need to curse out your creditors when calling you about the money you owe them. Just file Bankruptcy and geton with your life.

After I filed Bankruptcy, I was still in the process of my case being reviewed by the judge and was already getting things in the mail from car dealerships stating they could help me get into a brand new car. Even with my bankruptcy filing and once my debt was discharged, I was getting offers from all kinds of credit card companies who wanted to put me right back into debt, with a high-interest rate, but at least I had a second chance to redeem myself instead of trying to fight with all of my creditors who wanted to either sue me or garnish my wages. Filing bankruptcy was one of the best decisions I made financially. The second time around, I made better decisions and monitored my spending habits. You know, the things a responsible adult is supposed to do.

I look at Bankruptcy as the lifeline the government gives throws you when they were the very ones that pushed you off the boat, to begin with. I mean by this that the government allows us to obtain credit at the young age of 18 years old. The credit card companies are even set up on college campuses across the united states. This is a complete setup. Young college kids in the freshmen year are not responsible enough to take on significant debt. They haven't even passed their first economics course, and here come the credit card companies offering them a way to pay for things they cannot afford. This is absurd and should be banned. Now, this should fall into the category of predatory lending for sure. Since our government will allow credit card companies and lenders to prey on the young and irresponsible, it's only right they allow you to save yourself.

I am currently buying my own home, I drive a BMW, and it has only been five years since my Bankruptcy has been discharged. If I hadn't filed Bankruptcy all of the negative reporting and the lawsuits would still be going on today. I would have garnishments from creditors, and I wouldn't be able to purchase a home with the amount of debt I owed.

Bankruptcy is not for everybody, and it is best you review your finances thoroughly andmake the best decision for your financial situation.

Remember filing Bankruptcy will remain on your credit report as a public record for 7-10years, and you will pay more in interest for the items you buy. The upside is, you will prevent your creditors from suing you, possible wage garnishment, and several negative credit marks.

Remember, if you own property, a creditor can place a lien against your home, so to prevent all ofthese potential financial disasters, look into filing bankruptcy. You do not always need an attorney. As I mentioned before, I simply downloaded software, filled it out, and filed my Bankruptcy myself without the assistance of any legal authority. If you need help, feel free to reach out to me directly.

Chapter 10

What is a Charge-Off? And Should I Settle?

Simply put, a charge-off is a debt the finance company considers uncollectible.
This means the finance company has tried to locate their vehicle and was
unsuccessful, or the car was repossessed and was unable to collect the deficiency
balance, so they have to write off the debt. This happens right before it's assigned
to the third-party collection agency (the bottom feeders). I saved this topic for last
because it's essentially the last thing the finance company will do regarding your
account with them, and it's the shortest process of them all. The average time an
account is charged-off is around 120 days past due. This means the finance
company has tried for an entire four months to resolve the debt, and they must
either get the balance paid in full that day or write the debt off. Once it's written off,
this will report on the customer's credit report as a charge-off. The credit report
will still show the balance as owing, affecting the credit report negatively. This
debt does not go away, and you will still owe it. Don't let the term

charged-off allow you to think you don't have to pay it anymore. In fact, it's
the exact opposite. The finance company is charging off the debt and letting the
I.R.S. know it's no longer on their books, and they are forwarding all of the debt to
the customer, which will result in the customer receiving a 1099c from the I.R.S.

84

Yes, your taxes can be affected if an account is charged off. It's also possible to still receive a 1099c when you negotiate a settlement with a creditor and or collection agency, which means you will have to pay taxes on the unpaid amount.

Speaking of settlements, I'd like to say that a settlement can be extremely beneficial when trying to rebuild your credit and pay off your bad debts. The best advice I can give is to make sure you get it in writing before making a lump sum payment and never settle for paying more than 50% of the balance owed. If there is 600.00 or more left remaining on the debt you are settling, you will be paying taxes on it anyway. So be sure you take your best negotiation game with you when speaking with your creditors about the charged-off debt. Paying a lesser amount than what is owed sounds great, but you have to control the conversation and make sure you get what it is you need before you pay them. It is next to impossible to get a letter from them once you've already paid the debt off. Also, make sure you know how the settlement will report on your credit report. If they are simply going to put on your credit report "settled," it may not be worth paying. If they say they have to report the debt as settled once you pay it and pay no more than 30% of the debt owed. The only time a collections agency or finance company will not accept anything less than 50% is when the debt is new.

Older debts are easier to settle and negotiate. It's already been written off for years, and the finance company will be glad that you're at least paying something on it. The best tactic to use when negotiating a settlement is to pretend like you know nothing. If you call making demands and tell them you know what they can and cannot do, they will not cooperate. Just be nice, smile, and crack a joke or two, and no matter how much you owe, I am sure you will get a good deal on your settlement.

<u>Conclusion</u>

Getting into debt is easy and getting out is hard. Although this is the case, we don't have to become slaves to our debt. As a matter of fact, we can make our debts work for us. If you ever find yourself in financial hardship, please take advantage of the various programs I have discussed throughout this book. Also, be honest with them. What I noticed most about working with customers who were indeed in a real hardship were embarrassed to discuss their financial situation with a stranger. Still, the only way to get the assistance that is needed is to explain what happened. Finance companies are aware that at some point, someone is going to fall behind. It is in their best interest to offer assistance to keep their customers. All of the programs that I discussed were programs the companies I worked for used. There could be more options out there that I didn't discuss. If you ever get behind on your bills and there is simply nothing at all you can do, contact your finance company immediately, and they will offer you the assistance they have available. It's beneficial for both you and them to keep the account in good standing.

I know this information will help so many people, and I am happy that I was chosen to deliver it to the world. Thank You for your time.

Feel free to reach out to me on social media. I.G.: missteelane and Facebook T. Lane.

www.ingramcontent.com/pod-product-compliance
Lightning Source LLC
Chambersburg PA
CBHW040824300326
41914CB00073B/1673/J